Whiskey Stop Motion

poems by

Holley M. Hill

Finishing Line Press
Georgetown, Kentucky

Whiskey Stop Motion

Copyright © 2023 by Holley M. Hill
ISBN 979-8-88838-358-2 First Edition
All rights reserved under International and Pan-American Copyright Conventions. No part of this book may be reproduced in any manner whatsoever without written permission from the publisher, except in the case of brief quotations embodied in critical articles and reviews.

ACKNOWLEDGMENTS

Thank you to my sisters, Sarah and Katey, with whom I've shared so many stories. To Amy, Jess, Carolyn, and Stetson, my soul sisters, I appreciate and love you all. And for Alyza, because you are all the reasons.

Publisher: Leah Huete de Maines
Editor: Christen Kincaid
Cover Art: Holley M. Hill
Author Photo: Holley M. Hill
Cover Design: Elizabeth Maines McCleavy

Order online: www.finishinglinepress.com
also available on amazon.com

Author inquiries and mail orders:
Finishing Line Press
PO Box 1626
Georgetown, Kentucky 40324
USA

Table of Contents

Virginia, Reborn 1
Carolyn's House 2
Bathtime 3
Feeding Amy Whiskey 4
Plain Jane's Diner 5
Phony Magician 6
Black Eye Morning 7
Hit and Run 8
The Measuring Cup 9
Costume of the Invisible 10
Friday Night 11
Red Bug Getaway 12
Venice 13
Perfect 14
No Rules 16
With Me 17
Hydration 18
Letters to No One 19
Not Alone 20
21st Birthday 22
Sick Shepards 23
Rise and Shine 24
Demolition 25
Drunk Mom 26
Burning One Down 27
The Cashier 28
Dreaming in Drunk 29
Ax Handles 30
Author 32
A Late Tuesday Night 33
Gambling 34
Forget This Bar 35

Virginia, Reborn

I lie—
straight to his
face. *No, I
have not been
drinking!* But,
I've had nips of
Jaeger and wine
coolers, I forget
how many.

Does he know
me well enough
to call BS?
3 days now—
full of lies
empties,
desperation
and impulsivity.

I buy a six
pack, leave my
daughter in
the car while
I go in to pay.

She is still
wearing her PJs
and I drink a
whole can on
the way home.

Then I do
meth, discreetly
packaged into
little pills that
I pretend are
ok to take.

And I take
a lot. Enough to
make me shake,
forget things,
lie, pace, write
bad poems.

*I feel like
I'm married to
Virginia Wolfe,*
he says. *It's
always something
with you.*

When I look
offended all
he can say is,
*Well, at least
it's not
Syliva
Plath.*

Carolyn's House

The first time it was
Smirnoff Ice. One
12oz bottle of freezing
watered-down citrus
tonic that burned my
throat, an arctic cordial
smoldering the last
worn wall of my
childhood down to
ashes. We danced
in the driveway and
my cheeks hurt from
laughing and I
learned how to forget
everything that night.
If I had known it was
so easy, I would have
done it years
ago. My resolve to not
be my father, or my
ruddy faced stepmother had
held, a swollen barbed
fence until it swung open
and I was the last one
to drink. After the warm
forgetting fog started
to fade and I began to
remember, my forehead
found a door frame to
lean against. I stayed
that way, watching
my hands like a stranger
and all the curtains
I pulled shut when I
drank to forget opened
themselves without the
stage of drink. I was
helped to bed, crisply
made by unsuspecting
parents vacationing
in the naive comfort that
no drunken teenager would
cry herself to sleep between
their sheets. A lost girl
finding her first escape,
one drink still emboldened
in my belly, I knew,
right then, that it would not
be the last time
I would give up
and get drunk.

Bathtime

My body
knows when
to stop, but tell
my brain that.
Commanding chemical
tub, warm and
waiting, practically
steaming in the
cool air.

Who could resist
such a thing?
Not me.
Into drunkenness
I step, pulling it on
one foot at a time.

Zipped into
this alter identity
my reality wears
her suit of waxed
paper, all smudged
out and waterproof.

A cloak for chemists
or surgeons or
inmates. On me, a
jailbreak. My
superhero cape.
The very best
party dress.

And yes, when
costumed

in this idiotic
attire day after
day I get into the
bath with all
my clothes on.

Lean back, sigh.
Saturate. Sink
to the bottom
and drown.

Feeding Amy Whiskey

The night I got my
best friend drunk I
realized most people
can't drink as much
whiskey as I can.
She threw up in
our yard and I brought
her a mason jar brimming
full of water. She held
it, drops spilling over
glassy lips and then she
threw up again. I thought
back to our meager night
together, I thought of Anne
and that goddamn
raspberry cordial and the
fact that I must be
Ms. Shirley,
an influence as sour
as the taste in our mouths…
But who was I to
complain when my
best friend lay next
to me, blowing
chunks in the
bushes? So I helped her
to bed and tucked her
in and then I staggered to
the porch and instead of
sleeping I wrote and
I wrote until the sun
threw its collar over the
hills and I forgot, for a
moment, that I'd spent all
night getting my best
friend too drunk to simply
stay up and talk to me.

Plain Jane's Diner

The first time I dropped
acid drunkenness had already
tucked its scratchy black hat
over my eyes.
I saw the world as if
bending awkwardly
to peer through an unlit
keyhole. Swaying,
squinting, peeking
through slivers of
thick smudged paint.
I watched it happen
from the inside of my
eyelids like barred
up windows.

It was 2:00am. I think.
I was barefoot,
pacing the driveway, soaking
wet from lolling, floating
obliviously in the shallow end
of the pool.
I probably held tight
to a fresh drink.
I was thin.
I flirted.
My impulsivity misread
as courage and confidence,
like a sexy
too-tight mini skirt.

So when I popped
that tiny bone white
stamp between my teeth,
tonguing it per ritual
dictates, attention
inebriated my body—
hips pushed forward.

The next thing
I remember is coming to
at breakfast in a diner
I'd never been to
or even seen before,
towns away from where
I'd started.

My vision
suddenly focused,
clicked together
combination glasses
paned in layers of
lenses passing
control over
to the brain.

I think I ate some toast.
The colors on the walls
throbbed, too deep
to turn open eyes
away from. I think someone
in our small group
ate a huge plate of eggs.
The memory of his name
left the premises when we
left the diner and I
blacked out again.

Then I was in bed,
dried out and delusional,
writhing around in my
own sweat and confusion,
for two days.

When I finally recalled
the diner's name it was too
perfect to forget again.

Plain Jane's tables would
hold memories in the dark
for a decade, but I was still too blind
to remember I'd never even
paid my bill.

Phony Magician

Do you know
what a hangover
feels like?
Like showing
up at school
with fuzzy, unbrushed
teeth, dirty underwear,
mismatched socks
and no pants at all.

Like crashing
your bike after
blind flying
down a gravel
laid road—eyes
closed—mangled
metal skeleton
and dried blood
the only evidence
you were riding
at all.

Like contracting
food poisoning
after the best
meal you've
ever had, sweet
caustic taste lingering
in your mouth for days.

Like getting
caught, red handed,
in a hot white lie.

Like standing
in front of
an audience
playing at first
the role of a
skilled magician,
but then discovering

all your tricks
turn out to
be nothing
but smoke and
mirrors

Black Eye Morning

Stranded inside nightmare
lurks the unforgiving
memory of my knobby
cheekbone slamming,
the drop of a
bowling ball, against cool
blue stone sloppily tiled on my
mother's bathroom floor.
She wasn't there, of course.
We had been tossing shots
down our throats fast
for hours. I was plopped
atop the steely
washing machine, one
slippery giggle gone
too far when the bottom
fell out. After I hit the floor
I think I lay there, a
teenage bag lined with
bones and booze,
for a year. Sure-footed
boys rotated in, making sure
I was still alive,
I think. The bathmat was damp
and sandy. My words slurred,
tumbling on drunken ears. I just
wanted somebody to bring
me a blanket and
another shot, let me sleep...
The next morning I peeled
out, a smashed banana, from
warm twisted sheets
and I had forgotten
everything. When I looked
in the mirror, she
knocked me out with one
punch, and I was
the only one who joked
about the free fall that
left my face swollen and
greasy as a rotten grapefruit.

Two days later the blackout
turned to bruise, a shameful dark
bullseye, dead-center landmark
leading to questions
I simply didn't want the
answers to.

Hit and Run

Do you know
what a blackout
looks like?

Like a
photograph,
ragged,
furious white
space scratched
out where
your face
should be.

Like walking
into an empty
house—floor
stripped to
the bedrock,
walls unavoidably
bare and crusted
with thick
memories
that used to be
fresh and
smell like home
but now, there
is only the dirty
rancid stench of
deep dug holes,
a buried addition
of sloppy, dark
basement rooms.

Like being
shoved under
water at night,
blurred vision
a luxury. Humid
space between
frantic ribs,
chest unaware
of air, unable
to take another
breath.

Like going to the
movies with all
your friends,
oblivious of the
marquee that's slid
together with
letters that spell
out your name
along with the
title, "Not
a Happy
Ending."

Like walking
into a busy
street, eyes closed,
just waiting to
be hit. Waiting
to wake up alone,
somewhere unfamiliar,
no memory
of the car that
ran you over.

The Measuring Cup

The night wore her
summer perfume, cooing
noises rang out
of the trees; swamps sang,
bracken hummed fearlessly
—animals all electrified
drunken soldiers celebrating,
finally home, their time in cold
dark trenches lined with dark
earth all but a winter
memory. But we weren't
listening—we were
drinking.

I poured gin generously
into a scratched
glass measuring cup,
The first was
mouth cutting, crystal
clear vodka that made
the gin taste like nothing
but pine. After we drank
the cup dry, we talked each
other into adventuring.

The ride to the beach lasted
ten minutes, but I remember only
10 seconds. All of it held her eyes
bright, huge shit eating grin
across her flushed face, turned
to me instead of the road. After
we sloppily rolled through inky
dark waves, sighing, laying on
our backs, letting the lukewarm
surf soak our clothes
we looked at the spinning
stars, stomachs lurching and
decided to just go home.

The shower was as hot as
escaping death. We peeled
off our clothes like stamps
all used up, stripped from their
worn envelopes, and went into
the steam, naked, together.
Sand gathered into tide pools
at our feet that clogged the drain
and lingered between my
toes for days.

Costume of the Invincible

The fire tower was
much taller
than it looked
from the ground.

Shaking legs, slippery
rungs. One, then another as my
twin hollered, terrified and
determined twenty feet
below. I felt alive, huge,
elated. Who could
touch me up there?

Later, the train was packed.
Salem was prime real
estate on Halloween.
We had driven to the
train station but there
is no memory of driving
home. Red Jetta swerving
down affluent, ocean
lined streets. Guttural
laughter, silent blacked
out haze the same color
as that autumn midnight.

I spent the twilight lying,
weakly, on my dorm room
bathroom floor—mistakes
coughed up into the shower
until I couldn't keep my
eyes open anymore.

The next day, we woke
like dried out clams,
bodies tucked into
the roof of our mouths,
skittish in the light. All
I could think, lying there,
soaked in booze and
guilt, was *how had I*

*gotten down
from that tower?*

Friday Night

Always
one more
shot. Just to
get me good
and drunk. Well,
that didn't do
it. Maybe one
more, or two, or
cheers! Wait, that
was more than
one and I'm down,
from falling, ankles
tripped up by only
my own knees. Kiss
you? Why, your
lips are soft and thats
all the persuasion I—
am lost, where are
my friends? Lines
of people stare back
at my eyes glazed,
hurried from the
doors by hopefully
someone I know and
I know I am crying
and I know I need my
bed and then stumbled
feet crash, bra yanked
off as unfamiliar couch
moans when my body
drops between its arms.
Blackness. Oh wait, sun
light, and where am I? and
stale beer in my nostrils,
where's the bathroom, and
where am I? Familiar face
locked fingers, let's get out of
here. Shoes, shirt, cell phone,
where's your wallet? Press
lobby on the elevator
panel and then

take the walk of shame
through the yawning
streets of Boston
and wonder
what the hell
happened on
Friday night?

Red Bug Getaway

*No officer, we would never
drink and drive. We're
Mormon!* She held the
beer between her thighs and
stayed silent, as I suggested
when we were pulled
over halfway home from
Boston, both of us long
gone drunk. Wild eyes
full white and crazed. He
shined his flashlight in
the shadows, on our laps,
then decided we looked
way too innocent to
be what he had thought
we were. Flushed, doe eyed
pearl teethed girls, barely
women, who knew just
how to look at a man
and change his mind.

If only he
had known.

The next morning we
woke at home, in
the same bed, fists
clenched like we were
forcing something oily
thick and poisonous
from our palms. We
hardly spoke of it
at all.

But we laughed, and
thanked whatever God
there was for keeping
us alive and
out of jail
again.

Venice

The streets themselves
were like statues,
cobblestone buffed down to
a shine by a thousand years and
millions of moving feet. We ran
down them, cornered
lamplit mazes, uneven, illogical,
without any thought of an end,
which was fine by us because
our heads were wrapped in
wine; we might as well
have been blindfolded.
The cloudy, walled up water
was dull compared to the streets,
canals sang us their small, splashing
songs and we howled
crossing them, zig-zagging around
the palisade of San Marco Square, one
wide ocean eye watching us lose
and find ourselves a dozen times until
my ankle gave out;
I stumbled, stubbing
my buzz and my ego on the
bridge of Sighs, an ancient
gangplank who had seen
it all and been ground down
by the weight of it, becoming
a time worn statue in itself.

Perfect

Spotless countertops.
An empty sink.
Weeded gardens.
Stain free carpets
5 servings of vegetables and fruit.
A day.
Clothes folded, drawers closed.
Diet within daily calorie limit.
Dusted baseboards.
Sand free driveway.
Ironed outfit for every occasion.
Fresh flowers.
No cobwebs. Anywhere.
Empty laundry baskets.
Smiling baby. Fed baby. Changed baby.
Entertained baby with
educational activities.
Plucked eyebrows.
Shaved legs.
A body within my BMI.
Freshly painted walls.
Stark white refrigerator. Immaculate
Turned compost pile.
Mowed lawn.
Bed by 9.
No dessert.
Clean towels.
30 minutes of daily exercise.
Absolutely no booze.
Work on time.
Leave work late.
Glowing evaluations.
Exceeds expectations.
Bills paid. On time. All of them.
Say the right thing.
Wear the right clothes.
Never, ever cry.
Read. Every day.
Understand politics.
Dinner on the table.
Beds made.
Organized book shelves.
Clean windows.
Swept porch.

Teeth brushed. Twice a day.
Floss.
Vitamins, minerals, probiotics.
Agree. Compromise. Give.
Sex at least 3 times a week.
Wear sunscreen.
8 hours of sleep.
Just enough caffeine.
No candy.
Send birthday cards, buy gifts.
Say hello and smile.
Polished shoes.
Dry cleaned dresses.
A closet with full hangers.
Kale.
Walk the dog. Far.
Get a tan, not a sunburn.
Sing to baby. Laugh with baby.
Pristine, adorable nursery.
Cloth diapers. Organic wipes.
Recycle.
Return library books on time.
A bathroom floor you could eat off of.
Savings account. With money in it.
Labeled Pinterest boards.
Facebook friends.
Bikini line.
Get a hobby. Be good at it.
Make all appointments. On time.
Answer the phone.
Return calls. Write back.
Remember everyone's birthday.
Go out and have fun.
But not too much fun.
No hangovers.
No mistakes.
Wax. Tweeze. Trim.
Be loyal.
Stay calm.
Never, ever yell.
And, if you have time,
make sure the countertops
are spotless.
Again.

No Rules

Do you know what
a bender feels like?

Like being
kidnapped by
yourself,
in the company only
of an accidental,
raging case of
stockholm syndrome.
Before the blindfold
is even knotted, you
force yourself to throw
back the first of
many shot glasses,
syrupy medication
calming the frantic
woman caged,
strapped in her
handmade straightjacket.

Your hands are simply tied.

Like the discharge
of chambered fire
power—fingers cracking
home a weak trigger—taking
that risk of being
both the
bullet and
the prey.

Like spending
the night soaked in sweat,
releasing poison, breaking
a blistering fever that finally
lets you wake, only to drop
your spoiled body back into
inky sleepless rest,
bitter tongue a carpet,
taste of the sickness
that waits for you
behind restless,
crooked curtains.

Like causing a
shipwreck—memories
of tender, lapping waves
sucked to the
bottom along with
you, still clinging
pathetically to a broken
helm that never knew
how to steer anyway.
Panicked lungs
taking in water,
choking, coughing,
floundering in the
foul debris of hope.

Then finally,
popping to the surface,
a windy slap
to the face makes
thoughts snap
into place, you've
been destroyed—
floating aimlessly
the middle of
a forgotten sea

and you are very
much alone;
there is no land in sight.

Like taking a vacation,
and coming home
to war.

With Me

I only meander
ashamed, vanquished,
through the left
open garage
door when the
drink has relieved
the best of me.

My mouth starts
watering when I
think about liquor.
Is that normal?

Saying nothing but
silence—
speaks the loudest.

My twin's eyes,
blue, bright as fresh
acrylic paint
stare through me.

I am a window
and she has seen it all.

Or a mirror—I see her
see herself in
me. Conquered.

Between the damp,
slowly rotting
walls I smoke,
talk to myself

and think about
what she would say,
if she were here
with me.

Hydration

My teeth were
fuzzy. Tongue
like warm, cooked
meat. It was
hot. Damp fumes
of liquor clung
to the ceiling
and was the
only thing I
could taste, my
mouth flammable,
way beyond the
fire code. Someone
groaned. I unhinged
crusty eyelids, then
the moaning again.

I could feel the
cheap swaying of
a bunk bed—
somehow I had climbed
to the top bed, friends
laid out, motionless,
like stacked bodies
in a soon to be
morgue. My body a
corpse that could still
smell and hear the
heavy heels, dragging
to the small humming fridge
filled with college trappings.

My fingers
were traitorous
sausages, so I made no
sudden moves
for what I knew
I desperately
needed—hydration.

Instead I listened,
watched, envious
mouth watering as
the stuck tight seal
of the fridge let go
and she, purposefully,
in haste, pulled out a full,
unspoiled bottle of water.

But when my sour
jealousy peeked
and I saw her
unscrew the
cap, put her lips
around the rim, tip
her head back, eyes
closed, my envy
flung itself off the
bed in horror.

Immediately,
she spat, disgustedly,
not caring where,
and gagged.
Oh my god!
She shrieked,
half crying, *that
was vodka!*
I closed my
eyes, put my
fat fingers
on the sheets
and pulled
them over
my face.

I could wait a
while longer
for some water.

Letters to No One

There was an era of
notes. To no one but
myself.

Some neatly printed
ideas thoughtfully penned
during sober hours steeped
like my cups of guilt
inspired tea, stirred with regret
and the sugar of hope.

Other notes crammed
frantically with advice,
bulleted pleas and
sometimes I even
begged myself. Penciled
attempts to make a change,
while fully intoxicated,
to try to be a little
less crazy.

Friends had suggested
with encouraging smiles,
that maybe I
would listen to myself,
because I sure as shit
didn't listen to them
when they gave their
sad-dog-eyed talks,
late night words
to get me to stop crying.

It always began as I imagined
rouge waves would—quiet
depraved, moving swiftly and,
at the omniscient zenith,
foaming white with despair.

Then I took shots of anything,
holding on for dear life.

But, I knew by now to at least
try the life vest—give my
other, sober self
a small chance to live.

In the bathroom alone—
my only time out zone—
I unfolded the
premeditated yellowed
notes, glazed eyes waiting
for a reckoning truth. But after
reading what my own
hands had gifted me, I always
knew what really lay
between the lines,

a simply coded message—

notes could not
even begin
to solve
anything,

no, notes
could not save
me now.

Not Alone

I drink alone.

Like a guilty dog
chewing an expensive shoe,
when he knows
he absolutely
should not be.

But, it's always right there.
It's always right here.

I only buy strong liquor
Jaeger mostly, because
I'm not interested in taste
or counting calories or
searching for mixers.
I'm only interested in
one simple thing:
getting drunk.

I drive out of my
way to buy nips—start
throwing them back in
the car only to give
myself an excuse to
stop again and
buy more.

It's like re-uniting
with my oldest
friend, the one who
takes my mind out
of this place
for a little while.

The one who doesn't mind
being alone with me
for a little while.

21st Birthday

There was blood
dripping onto the
burnished bleach bone
bathroom tiles.
Someone dabbed,
heavy handed, with
a damp paper towel
at my face. Worried
words bounced off
the formica bathtub
and I was propped
up on the toilet,
jacket still halfway
zipped. Fumbling to
unlock the teeth and
shake it off, I noticed
my hands were rusty
no, bloody. Before
that moment I'd been
yammering things like,
I'm fine, and
it's just a little blood.
Seeing my greasy, street
clawed knuckles—suddenly
I remembered that
I'd lost my
shoes. My socks were
filthy, half torn off
so I tried to be funny.
Cue shit-eating grin:
*Does anyone have
my shoes?!* and
*Will someone bring me
a shot!?* Made up with
flushed cheeks,
slack jaw faces, my
girlfriends swayed in the
doorway, slipshot
glassy bird eyes
moving from my face to
each other. *What?*
I asked. My head started
to throb.
Someone handed me
a shot of vodka.
I threw it back—at
this point it might
as well have been
water. Sticky tart
streams rolled off
my chin. I handed
the thick bottomed glass
back over.

Holley, Carolyn
said, drawled out
voice steeped in
booze, she tried
to giggle but her
voice unrolled
like taught, wet panic,
look in the mirror. When
I turned my face, vision
finally focusing,
there was nothing
left for me to do but
cackle at the dark
eyed, old apple
wraith staring
blankly back
at me.

I wore a layer of
half dried blood
on my left cheek,
unfinished face
still being painted
by the inch-long
crushed worm gash
hung over my eye
with strung up
indignity.

My feet were
getting cold.

Later, I'd
learn we'd been
ungracefully
kicked out of
a gritty lacquered
bar—my sister and I
losing the group
instantly
outside in the
gummy, hot
stagnate air
of Boston's
late night
inner city.
She half carried,
half begged me
forward until my
thin socked toes hit
the sidewalk
and I fell over the
curb like a dead
tree, not even
able to brace
my ungainly fall. Neither
of us knew how doomed
I looked until a cab driver,
eyes squinting across the
street, yelled to
Sarah, *Oy, what happened
to you? Come, get in!*

I forgot who I was
when I woke up,
smothered into the
top bunk with Jess,
torpid, ethanol breath
hovering between
our dried out faces
and the too close
spinning ceiling. Then
I remembered. My
short twisted
dress was too tight,
rippled with cracking
dried up river beds
of blood. My drum beat
head out of rhythm.
Feet caked with
city-street dust,
nicked toed and naked.

I gagged on my first
thought,
*thank god for
sympathetic cabbies,*
and asked
*where the fuck
are my shoes?*

Sick Shepards

I notice that
every person
who sells
liquor suffers
the painful,
branded eye
of an executioner.

They receive
pitiful offerings
sacrificed atop
vinyl alters,
delusions of
slowly dying
souls nothing
more than a handful
of sweaty coins.

When I reach
the pulpit
I always bleat
gleefully.

Pretend I'm a
sheep in the flock,
unaware, oblivious
that I'm headed
towards the
slaughter.

Dutifully taking
my crumpled
bills those phantom
clerks with
haunted, herding
eyes simply pass
the knife over
to me.

Stockman stares
conclude the hot
iron branding,
mechanics move
split glass scenes,
the whole world
a slaughterhouse
behind such timid
walls help up
by gumptious
irony—

I am now
free to be both
butcher
and the
everwaiting

meat.

Rise and Shine

Do you know
what an eye
opener feels like?

That flying down
roller coasters feeling
your stomach
revels in when you
look upside down
at the sky
while swinging,
the ground churning,
weaving reality
with blinking threads
of faint haloed
lightheadedness
and bliss.

Like eating a mouthful
of honey straight
from the beehive,
angry bees hovering,
heat seeking, waiting
for retreat so they
can follow you
for miles.

Like telling your
parents that you
hate them when really,
you know, it's only
because you love them
too much.

Like singing your
favorite songs
so loud you
lose your voice,
just when you
need it most.

Like floating,
unknowingly
weightless and
careless, in hungry
eel infested
waters.

Like jumping
from a cliff, hearing
only the loud
rushing hot
air that makes
your eyes water
until there is
nothing
but blackout.

Like punching
through your
own coffin,

and waking
from the dead
to get up
and drink.

Demolition

My body is a temple
I must raze
to the ground, one
cold stone at a time,
plucked from weathered
seats mortared with
good intentions and
failure. It's cracked
alabaster hallways are
stained from clouds of
roiling smoke and lined
in cases filled with amber
jars all brimming over
with booze and
regret. It's doorways
creek on lusty hinges.
All the locks are
broken. Rooms hide
corners gathered with
dirty secrets and
lies, swept out of
way by sighs to make
room for the worn
down path ground into
the floor. It's foundation
cowers on chipped blocks
cut from the barren face
of the moon but even
these will give way
under the weight
of it all.

Drunk Mom

She slept in a
drawer that night.

Blue quilt clad baby
seemed only a sliver
of my life while I drank
till I could inhale
whiskey like
air.

The next morning
I took a shot
and packed her
like a simple
Christmas package
into my car. I
told myself I could
get home without it
but selfishness took
over and so carried
her—fish in a tank—
while I stood in line
buying liquor and
slurping it down
in the car like a
virus that paced
through her veins

silent as she slept.

Burning One Down

*Just go smoke a
cigarette,* he spits,
you'll feel better.

But I won't.
Not for lack of
nicotine, no—
I'll inhale plenty
of that venom,
rigorously exhaling
disappointment
edged with small traces
of self destructive
satisfaction.

Smoke signaling
the fact that I'm
doing a fine job
destroying myself
before anyone
else can.

I reply as steel
would, but broken.
Saying nothing
back to him, but
he's not even listening
anyway.

Too puffed up and
pissed off to stop—
see how I'm killing
myself, maybe just
to get his attention…

Instead of handing
back the same angry
words when he
looks away,

I just go outside
to smoke.

The Cashier

I always bring
my ID into the
liquor store because
he always asks.

And every time he
stops and states
*wow, you look
so young!* noticing
my overalls,
my pigtails, my
8 nips lined up
on the counter like
bullets being loaded
into their chamber
1, 2, 3, 4…

The woman behind
me won't make
eye contact and a thick
stench of ethanol
saturates the stale
air like radioactive
fallout. Antiseptic
aisles are silent
except for broken
bells, ringing out when
full glass bottles are
pulled from their
shelves, signaling
another safety
switching off.

Another victim
lined up ready
to cock their
own trigger,
arms full of nothing
but booze.

I leave, door
scolding me on
my way out,
and off in the
distance, I swear,

a shot rings out.

Dreaming in Drunk

We all had a
mouthful of
stories to inflame
our ruddy cheeks,
spiderweb the
whites of our eyes.
Wearing unruly
words like
fake tear drop
tattoos inked
with blackout
night time
nightmare,
only heard from
someone else
who reveled in
the telling, propped
up on a quivering
elbow. It felt like
retching; we spat
confessions onto
the dirty, sticky floor
fooling ourselves,
pretending
those cloudy damp
dream stories
were actually
foretold daydreams,
delusions of a
drunk living on
the cusp of
pretending and
the real.

Axe Handles

Do you know
what a relapse
feels like?

Like discovering
an ex-lover is
still infatuated
with you, letting
him ravage
everything and
anything you have
to offer, hot
guilt a storm
cloud between
your bodies.

Like swallowing
bile before you
step, knees
shaking
onto a rusty
circus ride, the
one that makes you
feel sick, but also
more alive
then ever.

Like dropping
extra weight,
stuffing pride
and soft
white belly fat
into your, "skinny
jeans," that you'll
wear until
midnight, when
a stranger peels
them off, thighs
like the handle
of axes, rattling
together as you
let him carve
into you. But
really, it's a mere
flesh wound.

Like Christmas
morning—giddy
anticipation smoldering
in your chest
until all the
carefully wrapped
up paper is
torn and
discarded, the
long gone surprise
now nothing
more than a
sick joke.

Like the first
swim of
summer—ice
out—courage
throbbing
through your
confused maze of
veins until
your limbs go
numb and you
start to sink,
drowning in
the weight
of a dead
sleep.

Author

I thought about
the resonant new
penny tinging
of jade bottles
heavy with
syrupy ink
disguised as
dark liquor
and wondered
if I could write
my staggering
story. I wanted,
so badly, to put
down my pen
burdened by
drunkenness and
let something
else, someone
else, roll out
that stained red
carpet in front
of me to make
sure I always
knew the right
way to go,
reveal words
worthy of
my desperate
plea for
empathy.

Late Tuesday Night

What I know is that
tonight I will
pace in the grass
and chain smoke,
talk to myself in
pensive voices, whisper
soliloquies with desperate
and barefaced speech.

I will write on the
walls, stay up too
late. I will listen
to melancholic
memoirs
empathize, sway to
heartbreak ballads.

I will haggle
feverishly
with words,
dictate
to my pressman,
a borrowed vintage
typewriter the
closest of friends,
personal printery
that never sleeps.

I will submit
poetry to whoever
listens, desperately
try to let go
of something,
anything, and shed
the burden of my
black cloud weight.

Then at dawn I will
pause, lift fingers
from lettered keys
and notice—

I'd made it
to Wednesday.

Gambling

After steeping
the raw lining
of my stomach in
sickly swallowed
back black liquor,
milky as venom and
just as strong

I salivate
and wait.

For me,
there is no
creeping up
of this feeling.

Fully charged,
it joyrides
through my
bloodstream,
broiling, enliving,
rallying the docile
troops to action.

Almost every time
I let out an
uncontrollable sigh.
God, that feels
so good.

I forget
in an instant,
peer reviewed
articles and
Alice in Wonderland
and all
common sense.

Reaching down
to unscrew
another thin tin
cap, clicking
reliably open like
flung wide gates
on a horse track,

I forget
everything
except for
cashing in
my ticket
worth nothing,
only cold stones
and bile
and dust.

Obliviously
unaware for one
small moment
that I had
bet the house
and lost.

Forget this Bar

The bar is polished,
ice cools tumbled
swills of potent
liquor; my mouth
is watering. Thighs
slide, feet kick the
greasy bottom rung
of a bar stool as I
go belly up. All day,
all year, every minute
holding on to every
second swallowed whole
by the want of it
and now here I am.
Fingers splayed atop
the silky lacquered coat
of oak, I part my
lips and bite my
tongue and cross my
toes trying not to drop
off the stool and
never stop falling.
The bar is slick
with bubbled rings
left from regret,
my hands retreat,
hide in my lap.
Eyes cannot shut,
will not abstain
so I see the tipped
up mouths, clear
and amber teeth clinking
in toasts to relief.
A question, so
simple, so easy to
ask, *want a drink, hun?*
The bartender wrings
out his soggy hands and
his words crash into
my body. Voice cracks
open with reply,
"ginger ale, please."

www.ingramcontent.com/pod-product-compliance
Lightning Source LLC
Chambersburg PA
CBHW040307170426
43194CB00022B/2934